THANKS!

Thank you to everyone who supported the creation of this book. We hope you enjoy it and learn something new!

A special thank you to Kathryn, who continues to inspire us with her endless creativity and wisdom, support, and care. We could not have finished this project without you. We are proud of you and all you've accomplished this year. This book is dedicated to you.

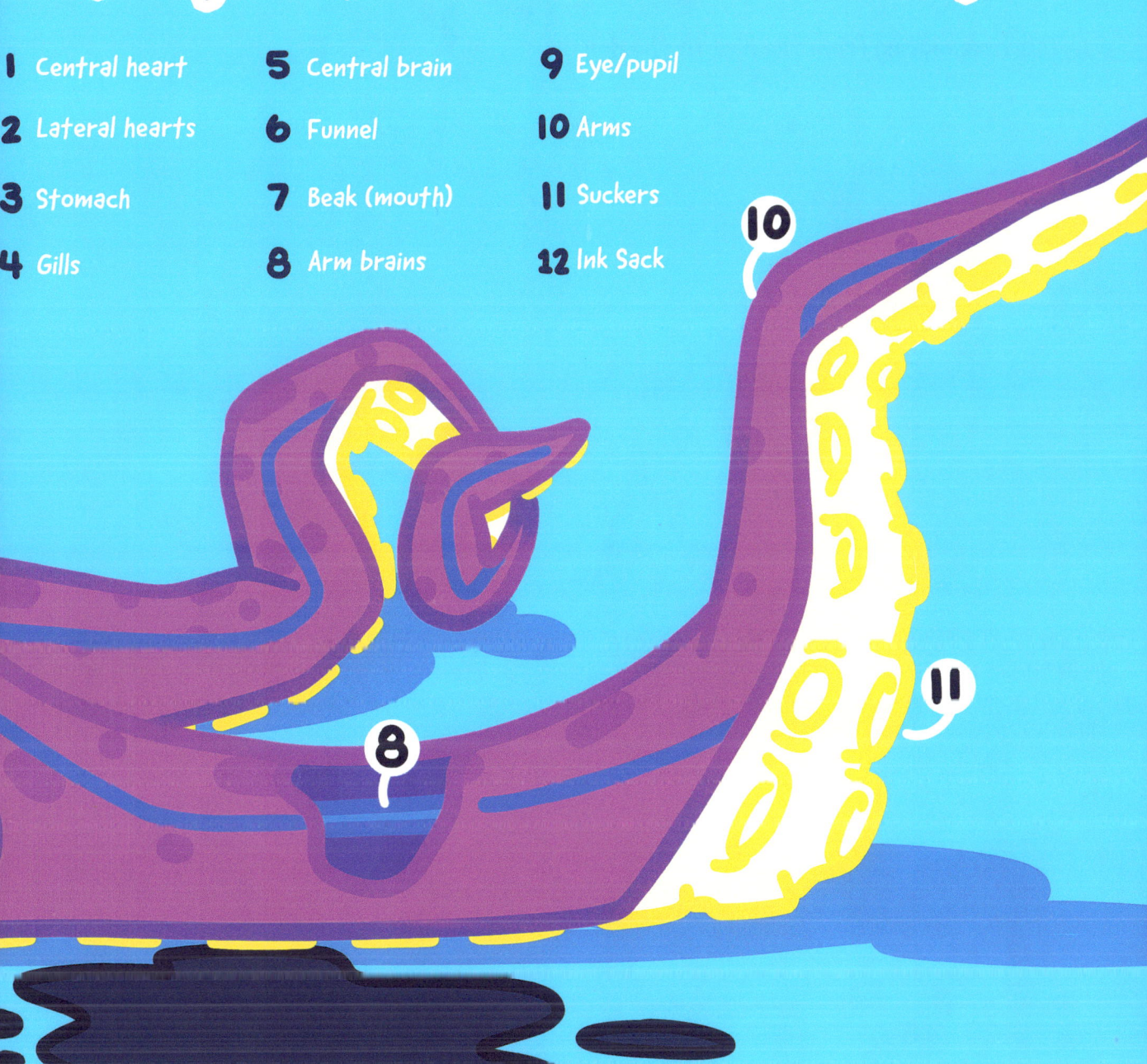

Fact: Octopuses hide in dens, which are typically cracks in rocks or other hard structures.

Octopuses live in the ocean, and when they get scared, shoot out a dark potion.

Fact: Octopus ink jumbles a predator's sense of taste and smell - it can even blind them!

Can you spot all seven of the octopuses hiding in this scene?

Fact: Muscles in their skin also grow and shrink to reveal pockets of colourful pigments.

With eight long arms,

and a big bulbous head too,

Fact: Octopuses' bodies contain no bones, so they can squeeze through very small spaces.

Their arms have many suckers,

to grab prey for their lunch,

Fact: Lunch may be shrimp, crab, lobsters, a variety of fish, squid, other octopuses, and shelled sea mollus

Fact: Octopus blood is blue because it has a copper-based protein instead of iron-based like humans.

Fact: Two thirds of an octopus' neurons are in their arms.

and one in each of their arms.

What a surprise!

Fact: Octopuses can feel, see, and taste with sensors at the ends of their arms.

they're found in every ocean,

along every coast.

Blue Ringed
Extremely venomous!
Up to 8 inches long.

Dumbo
Fins like elephant ears.
Up to 12 inches long.

Fact: Octopuses live in waters ranging from only a few feet to 13,000 feet deep.

Fact: While we often hear people refer to multiple octopuses as 'octopi', that is incorrect. The suffix "–i" for plural words only applies to Latin words. The word octopus is a Greek word, so the plural would be 'octopodes' if there weren't already an official English word: **octopuses**.

Fact: Octopuses can recognize different human faces, even if they are wearing a clever disguise.

Fact: Understimulated octopuses in captivity have been known to eat their own arms.

Fact: Cephalopod (squid, octopus, etc) is the Greek word for head-foot.

Fact: Females lay up to 400,000 eggs which they guard obsessively until the end of their life. They will even stop eating.

We hope you've learned
a couple new things.
Like never touch an octopus
whose skin has blue rings.

Or how these neat creatures
with their oddly shaped eyes,
will still know your face,
even with a disguise.

Now we must end
this informative book,
with one last rhyme,
and return to our nook.

CPSIA information can be obtained
at www.ICGtesting.com
Printed in the USA
BVHW020538151220
595404BV00004B/14